Discovering joy and tranquility
in the simplest pleasures.

First published and distributed by
viction:workshop ltd.

viction:ary™

viction:workshop ltd.
Unit C, 7/F, Seabright Plaza,
9–23 Shell Street, North Point,
Hong Kong SAR
Website: www.victionary.com
Email: we@victionary.com
 @victionworkshop
 @victionworkshop
Bē @victionary
 @victionary

Edited and produced by viction:workshop ltd.
Creative Direction: Victor Cheung
Design: Scarlet Ng
Editorial: Ynes Filleul, YL Lim
Coordination: Mavis Chan, Katherine Wong
Production: Bryan Leung

Cover illustration by Holly Stapleton

ISBN 978-988-75666-9-4
Printed and bound in China

LIFE
STILLS

Art & Illustration Inspired by Serenity

Welcome to a visual journey of happiness
in the little things.

Do you remember the last time you truly let your hair down, took a deep breath, and hit the pause button to listen to your surroundings? When we live in a world saturated with hurried footsteps, notification pings, packed agendas and the like, it can be hard to find pockets of peace and calm, let alone to stop and smell the roses.

Life is not meant to be filled with busy schedules and keeping up with deadlines, as the stress and anxiety that come with living a restless lifestyle cannot be more damaging to our mental health. To that end, buzzwords such as "mindfulness" and "self-care" have been springing up of late, promoting a new wave of awareness on the importance of improving our overall happiness through the likes of meditation, journaling, and connecting with nature.

While we are happy that these practices are being embraced, we have always been firm believers that finding and appreciating the good in all that is around us — no matter how tiny or insignificant it may seem — can also do wonders for the mind.

In this book, you will find brief moments of bliss and serenity immortalised into illustrations by 35 talented artists and illustrators who excel in capturing the subtle joys of the human experience. Although set against different backdrops and contexts, each piece of work also serves as a reminder that we are all connected across space and time through our shared existence and chasm of emotions — even if words escape them.

From a car cruising by the seashore near Mount Fuji to a lone skater practising ollies by the underpass, the city serves as the main subject in the works of Isao Aoyama (PP. 018), who invites viewers to explore the nooks and crannies of urban life. The architecture-centric work of Li Hyunwoo (PP. 026) offers canvases for contemplation through the play of light and shadow on close-ups of building exteriors, roadside railings, and stairwells, while the pastel neighbourhood portraits of Jack Mackenzie's (PP. 008) houses and estates paint a peaceful scenery of the suburbs with an inkling of nostalgia.

Akin to flashbacks of scenes from fading memories, the impressionistic strokes of agoera's paintings (PP. 101) elicit a dreamy glow with her depictions of people and objects in faded outlines and a sepia-tinged palette. On the other hand, artist Danny's (PP. 036) precise and detail-rich illustrations transport viewers into breathtaking nature-scapes via fir forests covered in a blanket of glittering snow or the flecks of light filtering through overhead trees along a countryside trail.

Just like the various portraits and stills of daily life catalogued within this book, beauty and solace can be found even in the smallest things that surround us. Be it through the fresh morning breeze, a steaming cup of coffee in the afternoon, or the serenity of a moonlit night, joy can be derived from the randomest places that we often tend to overlook.

When the opportunity next presents itself, why not delight in the comfort from a cat's purr or admire the resilience of a single flower growing through the pavement crack? You could even use the various words and expressions from around the world that we have included within this book as prompts for letting your mind wander. Paired with an illustration that echoes the same nuance of the word, we invite you to sink into the tranquil emotions each page evokes — so get comfy, dim the lights, and embark on a soul-soothing journey of LIFE STILLS, through which we hope you will be inspired to find snippets of happiness in your everyday.

agoera

Byun Young Geun

Caroline Péron

Clément Thoby

Danny

Dion Choi

for normal

Francesco Pirazzi

Frannie Wise

Gen Arai

Hezin

Hideki Kessoku

Hinako Goto

Holly Stapleton

Li Hyunwoo

Isao Aoyama

Jack Mackenzie

Jiatong Liu

Kazuhiro Takada

Kazuhisa Uragami

Kim Youngjun

Kohta Tomita

Lakitki/Woori Cho

Luis Mendo

Mari Kuno

Marie Muravski

Matt Saunders

Owen Gent

Park Hye

Sebin Park

Sosoon

Tatsuro Kiuchi

Youngchae Lee

Yukiko Noritake

Zao Ri

Jack Mackenzie is a Norwich-based artist who graduated with a BA in Fine Art (Sculpture) from Norwich University of the Arts in 2015. His pared-back, meditative drawings examine the aesthetics of domestic and commercial architecture — incorporating stillness, light, and shadow to create a sense of timelessness while exploring notions of nostalgia and memory.

Jack Mackenzie

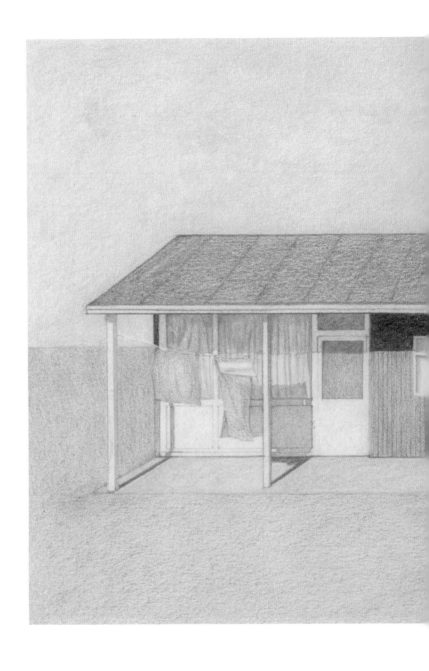

After living in Tokyo for many years, Isao Aoyama left for the seaside where he currently paints pictures every day. His paintings are coloured by the memories of his travels in cities and seas — local and far away. His main works are illustrations for magazines, book covers, and collaborations with apparel brands.

Isao Aoyama

isao. Aoyama

Li Hyunwoo is a Korean artist who is inspired by moments in daily life to encapsulate simple yet unexpected beauty on a rectangular canvas. His unique style features redefined colours and shapes from his vision, through which he creates an interesting rhythm and a touch of abstractness using texture and temperature.

Li Hyunwoo

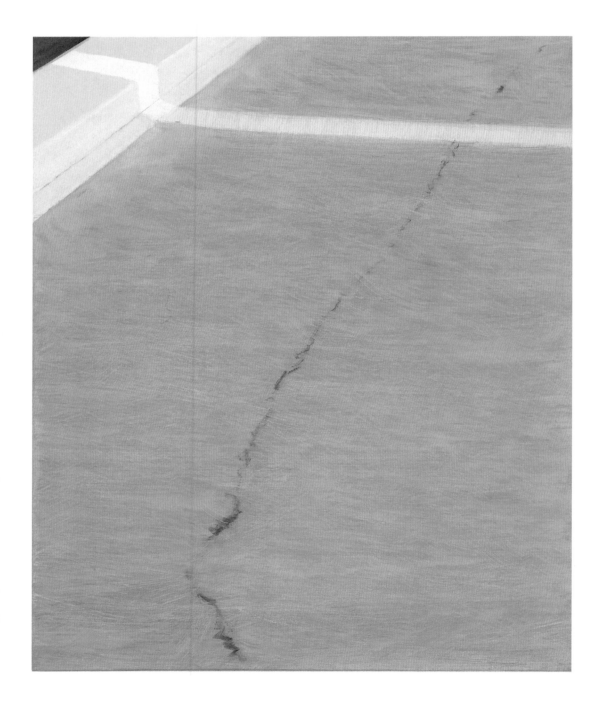

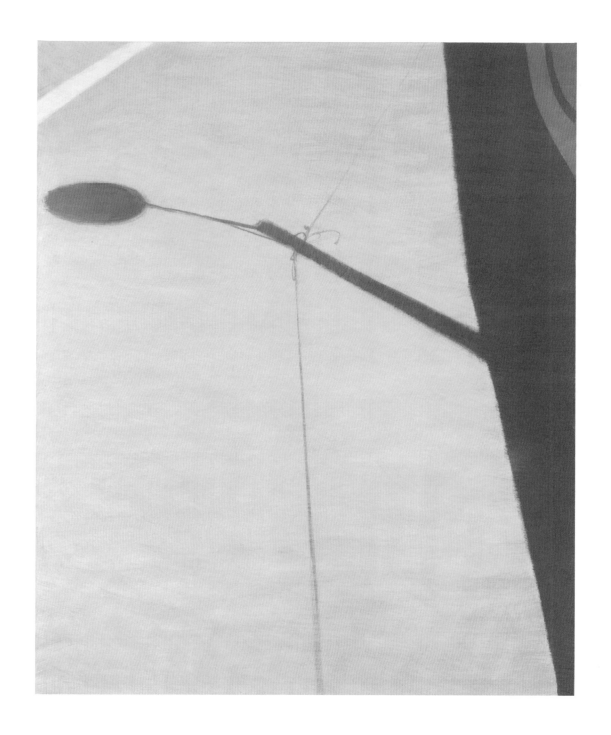

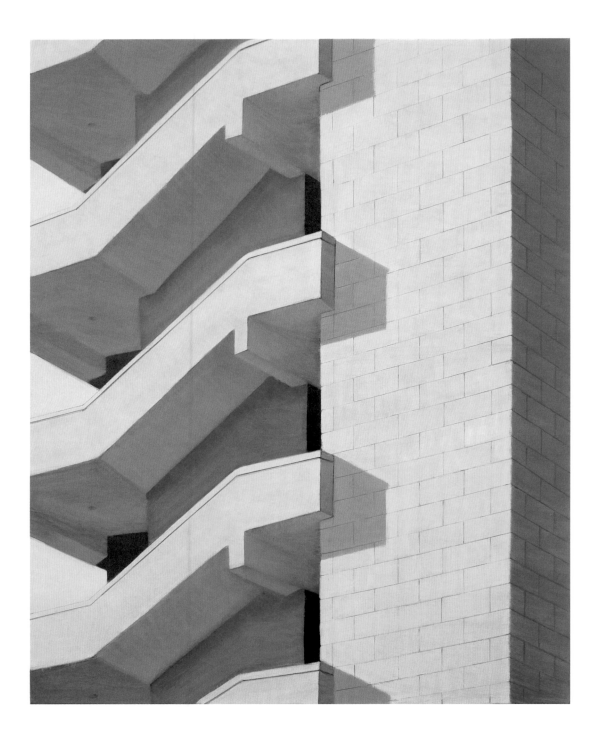

Born in 1987, Danny is a Japanese illustrator based in Osaka. Upon graduating from Kyoto Seika University in 2010, she began her career as an illustrator by focusing on client work. Her love for nature is reflected in many of her original illustrations.

Danny

Byun Young Geun is a watercolour artist, illustrator, and graphic novelist. Currently based in Tokyo, he produces illustrations for publications, books, and album art. Every year, he releases a graphic novel capturing our everyday existence enveloped by cities and the natural world.

Byun Young Geun

物の哀れ

/mònó nó áwàrè/ *noun* [Japanese]

Fondness for what is or will be gone and a sense of
calm for what lies ahead

Lakitki is the pen name of Woori Cho, an illustrator living in the countryside who enjoys walking and the colour green as they offer feelings of calm and comfort. Lakitki also believes that happiness can be found in life's unexpected moments and tries to capture them through paintings.

Lakitki/Woori Cho

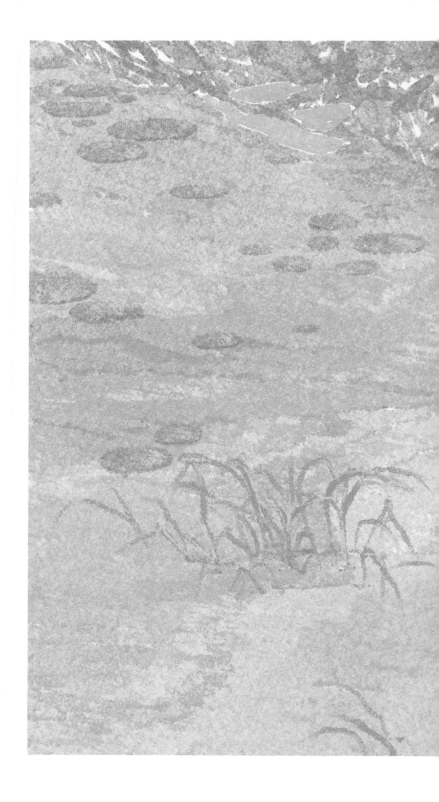

Zao Ri is a freelance illustrator whose work revolves around capturing the delicate moments between everyday life and daydreams. She uses warm, textured touches to create soft and poetic spaces in her art. She also explores illustration as a visual language in order to explore new possibilities.

Zao Ri

Hezin is a Korean painter and illustrator who specialises in drawing shapes of the mind found in everyday spaces. She majored in spatial design at university and had two solo exhibitions in Seoul. Most of her paintings are indoor scenes in a calm and quiet atmosphere, depicting the preciousness of alone time and the desire for peace.

Hezin

Dion Choi is a Korean illustrator based in Auckland. His illustrations challenge people to go beyond their physical realm, transported by their endless self-interpretations into another surreal world. Incorporating elements of art therapy, his work is often described as therapeutic, resilient, and surreal.

Dion Choi

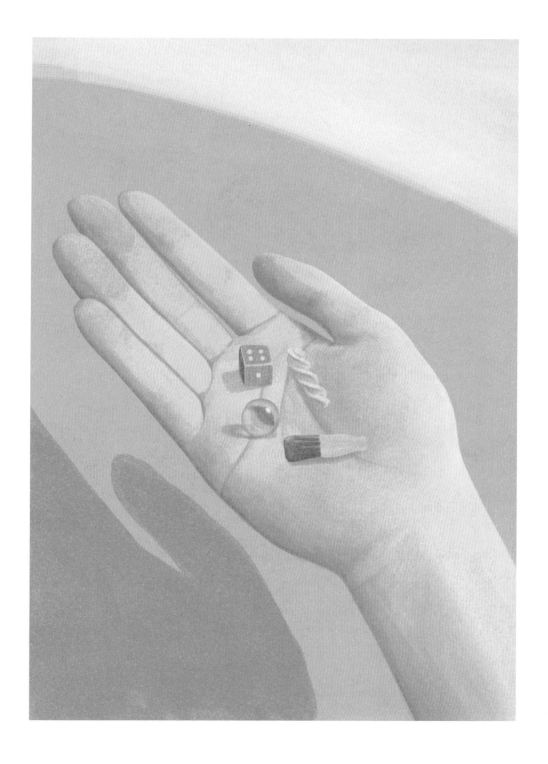

073

for normal is the pen name of Park Hyunjung, who has held a solo exhibition entitled "Drawing Thoughts" and had their works showcased at "The Colour Spot", a Seoul-based art exhibition. Hyunjung enjoys capturing daily moments like reading or going for a walk in their art, and plans to publish a drawing essay and open an online arts goods store in 2023.

for normal

βόλτα

/vólta/ *noun* [Greek]

A leisurely stroll in the early evening or at dusk
after a day's work

Kim Youngjun is a painter and media artist who presents the moving image as completed work. After graduating from Hongik University, he participated in various group exhibitions and held a solo exhibition at Gallery Meme. He has collaborated with brands such as Big Hit Music, LG oled TV, and Naver.

Kim Youngjun

Sosoon is an illustrator who also works in motion graphic design. Sosoon's paintings usually focus on landscapes, cityscapes, and elements that can be easily found in daily life. By featuring the familiar and ordinary, Sosoon hopes to touch people's hearts with cherished memories of the little things.

Sosoon

Park Hye creates with the desire to depict scenes from daily life with sincerity. She captures the beauty in the little things as well as nature by seeking them, underlined by her belief that painting them can add a touch of warmth to even the most ordinary moments.

Park Hye

Born in Shizuoka and currently based in Kanagawa, agoera graduated from the
department of graphic design at Tama Art University as well as MJ Illustrations.
He works with acrylic paint on plywood and uses everyday landscapes and people
as motifs, aiming to capture various atmospheric feelings in his work.

agoera

Youngchae Lee is a Korean illustrator who lives and works in Gyeonggi-do. She enjoys observing vast landscapes, watching people go about their daily lives, and producing illustrations inspired by these things. She published her second collection of work, "Alone Time — Here and There", in 2019.

Youngchae Lee

雲淡風輕

/yún dàn fēng qīng/ *adjective* [Chinese]

Directly translates to good and breezy weather; also
describes feelings of nonchalance and lightness after
going through a rough patch in life

Clément Thoby studied applied arts at the Estienne school in Paris and specialised in animation cinema at EMCA of Angoulême. He currently works as an illustrator in international press, communication agencies, and branding. His work mainly consists of imagined and real landscapes from his travels.

Clément Thoby

A graduate of the department of illustration at Aoyama Juku, Hinako Goto is an illustrator based in Tokyo whose work features light as the main theme. Honing a variety of illustration styles, including digital realism and comic art, Hinako always illustrates with the aim of telling a story.

Hinako Goto

After graduating from Takushoku University with a major in industrial design, Fukushima-born Kazuhiro pursued illustration at Aoyama Juku and became a member of the Tokyo Illustrators Society. With landscapes of daily life as his inspiration, he mainly uses acrylic to create works that connect to the viewer by evoking stories through memories and the imagination.

Kazuhiro Takada

A 2021 graduate from Arts Décoratifs de Paris, Caroline Péron is a Paris-based illustrator who works with press, publishing, and advertising companies. Drawn to the atmosphere of summer, luminous bodies, and wooden landscapes, she enjoys creating personal and commissioned work using coloured pencils. She published her first graphic novel, "À la recherche de Jeanne", in 2022.

Caroline Péron

138

Ćeif

/chayf/ *noun* [Bosnian]

Slow and silent enjoyment of an activity or the
company of another; a pleasure that brings relaxation
and calmness

Frannie Wise is a painter and illustrator based between London, Northumberland, and Edinburgh. Influenced by nature and the soft landscapes from her childhood, she infuses warmth and movement into her dreamlike paintings — depicting reality and half-memories combined with folk tales and characters based on the location.

Frannie Wise

144

146

Holly Stapleton is a Toronto-based illustrator and painter whose style focuses on merging the analogue and the digital. She enjoys capturing scenes in bright, golden-hour light using gouache textures. Through her editorial and commercial work, she explores the complexities of the human experience underlined by themes of selfhood, relationships, and nostalgia.

Holly Stapleton

Jiatong Liu is a Chinese-born illustrator living in London. Although he has just started out in his career, he has won several prestigious awards for his work and has developed a distinctive style that reflects what he sees in his wildest dreams, manifesting the world from his imagination into unique outcomes.

Jiatong Liu

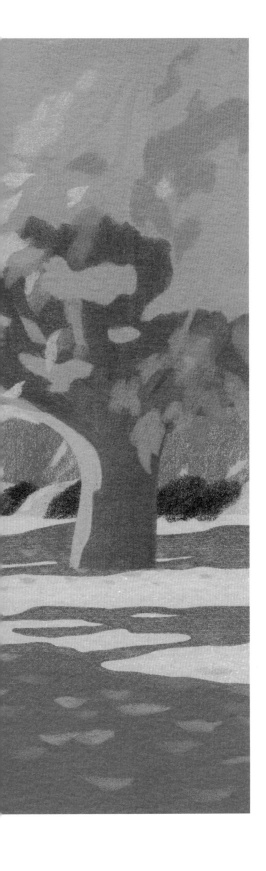

Mari Kuno is a Kanagawa-based illustrator who graduated from the department of design of the Nagoya University of Arts and Sciences. She paints and creates illustrations for advertisements, goods, books, picture books, and more. She has also held solo exhibitions in Tokyo and overseas.

Mari Kuno

kunomori

167

Flâner

/fla-ne/ *verb* [French]

The act of aimlessly wandering without any
destination, just to enjoy the view

Tokyo-born Tatsuro Kiuchi switched to a career in art upon graduating with distinction from the ArtCenter College of Design. He illustrated for children's books with US and Japanese publishers, before branching into editorial, book jacket, and advertising commissions. Owner of the PEN STILL WRITES studio and a Tokyo Illustrators Society member, he also teaches illustration at Aoyama Juku.

Tatsuro Kiuchi

Kohta Tomita is an illustrator and designer from Numazu, a seaside town in Shizuoka. After graduating from Musashino Art University, he began creating illustrations for corporate advertisements, books, and food packaging designs. In his work, he expresses the atmosphere of daily sceneries such as small harbours, embankments, and fishermen — inspired by the place where he was born and raised.

Kohta Tomita

Matt Saunders is a London-based freelance illustrator whose art is often rooted in bringing fantastical yet calming atmospheres to life and solving visual problems through unique images. He has worked extensively in the publishing, design, and advertising worlds — creating everything from book covers to billboards for clients ranging from tech companies to Broadway.

Matt Saunders

Gen Arai is a freelance illustrator, painter, and artist who has been awarded by various organisations and publications. He was the selected winner of American Illustration AI41 and the merit award in the 3x3 Illustration Annual No 18 in 2022. In 2021, he was the selected winner of American Illustration AI40 and received an honourable mention in the 3x3 Illustration Annual No 17.

Gen Arai

192

Friluftsliv
/free-loofts-liv/ *noun* [Norwegian]

The joy of being outside/spending time in remote
locations for one's spiritual and physical well-being

Based in Tokyo, Kazuhisa Uragami studied in Aoyama Juku under illustrators Tatsuro Kiuchi and Zenji Funabashi. As part of PEN STILL WRITES, he is now an illustrator himself — working for a wide range of books, magazines, music projects, and advertising. His work has been recognised and awarded by American Illustration and the Society of Illustrators, to name a few.

Kazuhisa Uragami

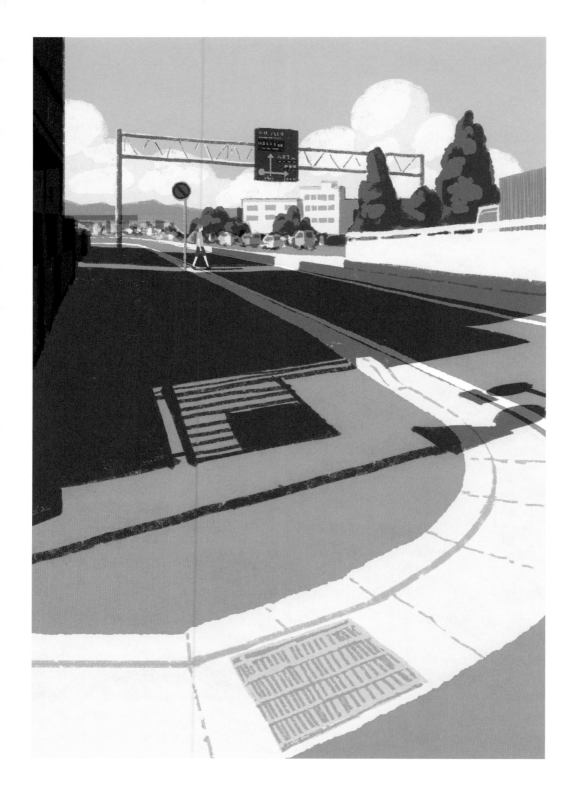

After 20 years as a creative director in Europe, Luis moved to Tokyo to pursue a career in drawing. His illustrations can be found on websites, magazines, advertising, galleries, and clothing, and his clients include Apple, Forbes, and Monocle, to name a few. Luis is also the creative director of artist residency Almost Perfect, which he co-founded in 2018.

Luis Mendo

Born in Kanagawa in 1974, Hideki Kessoku is an illustrator who graduated from the department of design at Tokyo Polytechnic University. He is a member of the Tokyo Illustrators Society and Japan Graphic Designers Association, and mainly works in advertising and illustration for books, picture books, and theatre posters.

Hideki Kessoku

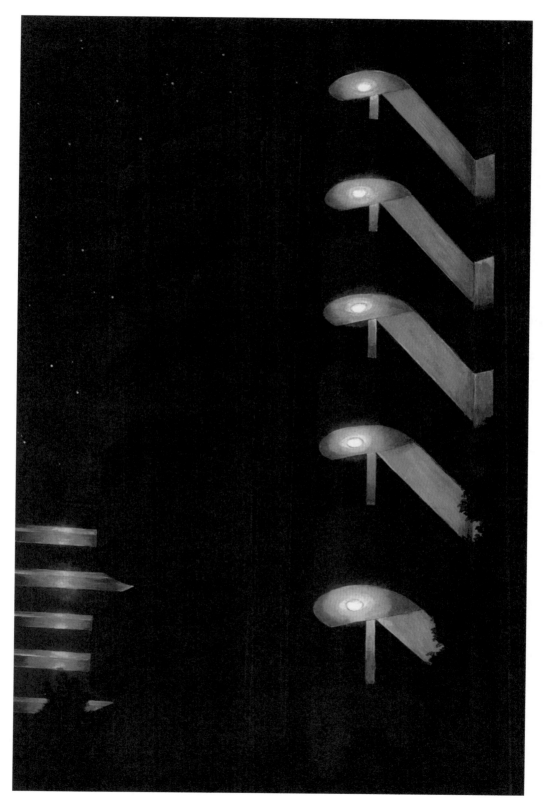

Owen Gent is a Bristol-based illustrator who works on book cover designs, editorial illustrations, charity campaigns, and children's books. Combining traditional painting techniques with a contemporary style, his work approaches subjects with delicacy using colour, depth, light, metaphor, and figure. His clients include The New York Times, The New Yorker, Penguin, The BBC, The Economist, New Scientist, Vogue, Amnesty International, TED, and The V&A.

Owen Gent

мѐра̄к

/mèrāk/ *noun* [Serbian]

Pleasure derived from the simple joys of daily life

Marie Muravski graduated from the Seversk Art School in graphic design before studying illustration in the Czech Republic. As a book illustrator for over 8 years who has collaborated with publishing houses, self-publishers, writers, as well as musicians worldwide, she is experienced in creating silent stories, comics, and animations. She also produces artwork for Voroh Studio's computer games.

Marie Muravski

Marie Muravski

Sebin Park graduated from Hongik University majoring in oriental painting. His work has been showcased in multiple exhibitions since 2016, including the 1st and 5th Seoul International Art Shows, This or That (2021), and the Starfield Art Festival (2022). He also produces artwork for albums, book covers, and postcards.

Sebin Park

230

Born in Aichi, Yukiko Noritake is an illustrator and artist based in Paris. Upon graduating from Ecole de Condé Paris in 2018, she launched her illustration career with "Voyage au Pays des Odeurs (Actes Sud)" — her first book and final year project. Since then, she has been honing her style through a variety of artistic endeavours using her medium of choice: acrylic paint.

Yukiko Noritake

238

Waldeinsamkeit

/vahyd-ahyn-zahm-kahyt/ *noun* [German]

The feeling of being alone in the woods and at peaceful
oneness with nature

Francesco Pirazzi graduated from the Academy of Fine Arts of Florence in 2018 at the Painting School of Adriano Bimbi. Born in Veroli in 1994, he currently lives and works in Turin. His work has been exhibited in multiple group exhibitions at galleries in London, Siena, Fiesole, and more. His last solo show "Somewhere Else" was curated by Cristoforo Maria Lippi at Augustenborg_Project.

Francesco Pirazzi

Index

P. 245
Torre
Oil, canvas
550 × 400 mm

PP. 246–247
Conversazione
Oil, canvas
870 × 640 mm

PP. 248–249
Attraverso la notte
Oil, canvas
1000 × 800 mm

Acknowledgements

We would like to specially thank all the artists and
illustrators who are featured in this book for their
significant contribution towards its compilation.
We would also like to express our deepest gratitude
to our producers for their invaluable advice and
assistance throughout this project, as well as the many
professionals in the creative industry who were generous
with their insights, feedback, and time. To those whose
input was not specifically credited or mentioned here,
we also truly appreciate your support.

Future Editions

If you wish to participate in viction:ary's future projects
and publications, please send your portfolio to:
we@victionary.com